Healing The Feminine Energy:

& The Wounds of Your Inner Child

By Reemus

COPYRIGHT

TABLE OF CONTENTS

Table of Contents

INTRO

Traits of The Feminine

The Wounded Feminine

- Passive person or people pleaser
- Seeks external validation/needy
- Emotionally withholding *or* overly emotional
- Victimhood and feeling of powerlessness
- Manipulative
- Insecure
- Envious
- Judgemental
- Struggles to receive or let go of control

The Empowered Feminine

- Peaceful
- Not easily triggered
- Expresses creativity

- Able to express authentically and
  communicate boundaries & needs
- Balanced and authentic expression of
  sexuality and sensuality
- In touch with intuition
- Emotionally balanced
- Cooperative

In this book, we're going to take the first steps towards healing your feminine energy. We'll start by describing the nature of the feminine spirit, and then we'll discuss what causes wounds to this energy and how to unblock the obstacles to its expression.

While this book is directed at women, it is not exclusively useful to women. Both men and women have feminine energy within them – albeit at varying levels – and we must all look after it. It is also useful if a man wants to better understand the energy of women, so he knows what a spiritually healthy woman looks like.

There are two main focuses in this book: 1) wounds and 2) blocks to the feminine energy. The first task is to identify any wounds, and this is done by looking back into your past. The next task will be identifying blocks, and this is done by embracing the present moment. Though closely linked, they are still separate, and one area may be more necessary for you to work on compared to the other.

Going on this journey of feminine development will lead to great fulfilment as you grow into a truly empowered person who is at peace with yourself, and in love with your nature. Now, let's get started.

The Spirit of the Feminine

If I were to ask you *"what is it that you use to touch, feel and interact with the world?"*, you may tell me that you use your body, and you wouldn't be wrong. But when it comes to the experience that you have here in this world, your physical body is only one part of it. There is much more to it.

Aside from your physical body, you also have a spiritual body. Your spiritual body houses and expresses your energy, and it is just as significant as your physical body. If you want true fulfilment, then both your physical body *and* your spiritual body must be in a healthy, balanced state.

Inner satisfaction is achieved when you align both the physical and spiritual body. They must be in unison. This means that the energy you express must match the design of your physical body. This is where masculine and feminine energies come into play.

If you are a woman, then feminine energy is the match for you. And for men, it would obviously be masculine energy. Of course, no person solely expresses one or the other. There is supposed to be a balance between the two. However, each person has either a 'feminine core' or a 'masculine core'. In other words, you will find that one energy is more prominent in you than the other.

In this book, we are focusing on feminine energy, and it is something that is inherent in all women. The female body was designed to express femininity, so it comes naturally to most women. Traits of femininity include openness, trust, magnetism, intuition, compassion, gentleness, creativity, and vulnerability. These are all traits that naturally come from the feminine energy.

The beauty of being in your feminine energy is that you will feel aligned, fulfilled, and whole. It is for this goal that you should embark on the journey to rediscovering your femininity. But taking it further, you should stop now and ask yourself: *Why do I want to go on this journey?*

What is it that pulls you to want to heal my feminine energy? The answer to this question will be the fuel that motivates you. It has to be more than just "it's a trend", or "it sounds interesting."

You must look at this journey as the start of your feminine development. It's a journey and the benefits will be rewarding. In this book, the aim is to heal your spiritual body so you can embrace your true state.

Your Inner Child

Every one of us, man, or woman, has an inner child. Now, that inner child is a perfect representation of your energy, because the spiritual body does not age. It is only your physical body that wrinkles and grows old. That inner girl you have deep within is your pure feminine state, before all the experiences, cultural programming, and traumas that caused her to hide.

If you'd like to understand how true it is that the 'child' within is pure in its masculine or feminine energy, simply observe children in the playground. Children are a great example, because they have not yet received social conditioning and hurtful experiences that affect their energy. They run entirely off pure energy. You can clearly see how masculine or feminine energies manifest through how young boys and girls interact.

Your inner child is the same way. That little girl inside is your feminine spirit. But if she has been attacked, it's likely that she'll struggle to come out and play like the kids in a playground. The playground for adults is not as innocent as the ones in kindergarten. Depending on your personal circumstances, there will be different reasons why that little girl was hurt.

Experiences that cause wounds to your feminine spirit can include mistreatment, neglect, abuse, heartbreak, trauma, or criticism. You could be a girl who has had no trouble being in your feminine energy until one of those situations happen. And it could be from one momentary but hurtful experience (like being badly treated in a relationship), or it could be after a long-term experience (like a rough childhood).

However, it may not even necessarily come from bad experiences like this. A girl might feel her feminine energy is blocked because of cultural programming. Unfortunately, we do not live in a world that respects femininity. Due to emergence of feminism over the last century, young girls enter a world that shames the expression of feminine energy and discourages them from embracing the role of a woman.

Regardless of whether it was from personal experiences or cultural programming, the result for most women is the same: *there is a struggle to embrace the feminine energy.* What happens when the little girl inside is hurt? The protectiveness of the masculine energy emerges. Note that this is also the thing that pushes men to be protectors. But remember, masculine energy is within women too.

So, when your feminine spirit is under attack, the masculine energy comes out to protect it. It begins to form a shell that guards the little girl. After she suffers wounds and cuts, the little girl is scared to come out and play, so the masculine shell remains. And since the little girl has not been healed, the pains suffered in her past will remain.

Even worse, operating on pain will become a regular part of your identity as you reaffirm over and over that the hurt version of yourself is who you are. Your thoughts, beliefs, and expression become aligned with the distorted expression of the masculine energy. Initially, being in your masculine energy will feel necessary and maybe even satisfying. But it will soon become exhausting because this is not the natural state of a woman.

Feminine development starts with healing your feminine energy so that you can feel royal, powerful, and confident. Femininity is a woman's greatest strength and tapping into it provides a buffet of benefits, and it's available to every woman who wants it.

You may be waiting for someone else, perhaps a man, to come and do the work for you. But if you do this, now you are at the mercy of other people to decide whether they will grant you the pleasure of being the woman you deserve to be.

The immature expression of femininity is passiveness. This type of woman waits and allows life to happen *to her,* rather than *for her.* But you don't have to wait for someone to make things better. You can do it too.

Femininity is already in you; you just have to get it out. All you have to do is decide that you deserve to be the woman you desire to be.

INSECURITIES

The feminine state is based on internal 'being', whilst masculinity is a state based on external 'doing'. The more internal work you can do, the better for the feminine spirit. A woman is going to struggle to enter an internal state if there are painful wounds that lie beneath the surface. So, healing past traumas and insecurities are very important because fears will trigger the protective response of the masculine shell to emerge.

The feminine energy needs to feel safe. By addressing problems of the past, including prior relationships, family upbringing, and any other relevant areas, we begin to create comfort and security that allows the feminine energy to flow. This requires being truly honest with yourself.

So if you can show a great level of accountability in this area, you have much to be proud about. One of the main goals is to reach a place where you can just 'let go' of attachments to all triggering thoughts and insecurities.

Get to Know Your Inner Girl

The first task to healing your wounds is getting to know the little girl inside. When you strip away all the painful experiences you have endured, who are you? Who are you before all the societal conditioning, family criticism, or abusive relationships? Who is that little girl within, in her purest state without all the overthinking, the overanalysing, or constant worrying?

In a world of total safety and freedom, who is she? And trust me, she's in there. We just need to let her know that it's safe to come out. She needs to know that you're here for her and you're going to keep a watchful eye over her. She needs to know you care.

She may have suffered wounds, but you're here to help her heal them. Now, what is the first thing you must do when you suffer a wound? You must assess it and clean it. If not, it gets infected, and the healing process becomes complicated. That is much like what has happened to all of us in this world.

Most of us have grown up without cleaning the wounds to our spiritual bodies. We left it as it is. And unlike a physical wound, you don't go to a hospital and get it bandaged. There are no scanning machines and X-rays to assess the damage done to the little girl within.

Those scans are going to have to be done by you being vulnerable and honest. We must go back and look at your past to see when you suffered those wounds so we can get it all cleaned up. We may have to go back far but it will all be worth it.

Assessing the wound

Wounds to the feminine spirit usually occur after you suffer the type of experiences that lead to a feeling of shame, blame, regret, or lack of confidence/insecurity. And these negative mental states can lead to suppression of the expression of a number of areas, including:

- Body image & beauty

- Love & sex

- Emotions & personal expression

- Self-worth & personal value

For example, if you've been in a relationship where a partner frequently criticised how you look, it may lead to a *lack of confidence* in how you view *your body*. Or, if in your childhood, your parents used to make you feel stupid when your grades were not good enough, it may have caused you to feel *shame* and not *worthy* of praise.

You must be vulnerable and think back to what it was that caused any mental scars. Sit down, close your eyes, and really play the scenes back in your mind. Have you experienced abandonment, scorn, neglect, or rejection?

Be honest with yourself. It may hurt a little bit as you recount those memories and that's okay. Once you have identified the different wounds you have, you must then observe the long-term effect it had. Ask yourself: what beliefs did you retain from those negative experiences?

When you have negative self-thoughts or certain beliefs about your sexuality or your emotional expression, where did those thoughts come from? Did someone else put them there and are they in a position to do so? What validated them to be able to plant certain thoughts in your head? And when they did so, was it done with good intentions? Many of the thoughts you have are not yours and were planted there. And those weeds are suppressing your feminine spirit.

Continuing from the example in the previous paragraph, perhaps you may have loved your body before being with a partner that criticised it but now you hate it. The worst thing is not the criticism itself. It is the self-acceptance of that criticism as you replay it over and over in your head. So even after that relationship is finished, those same thoughts persist. You have given power to the negative affirmations that they gave you.

Now, when you take off your clothes, you feel a sense of *shame* or *lack of confidence*. You tell yourself that you hate your body and wish it was designed differently. You scroll on social media watching other girls' bodies wishing you could look like them. You don't know it, but you are hurting that little girl inside when you do this. It's hard for your feminine spirit to thrive when you are continuing the verbal abuse that you suffered in the past.

EXERCISE

Journaling: It's time for some self-love to replace the negative affirmations of your past with positive affirmations. Make a commitment to let go of any shame, blame, regret, or insecurity.

In each of the areas we spoke about above (body/beauty, sex/love, emotions/expression, self-worth), write something you love about self. Do this every day. For example, write one thing you love about your personality (which is a form of expression). Then the next day, write one thing you love about your body. It doesn't have to be major.

Process The Past

Among the most important aspects of healing
are *acceptance* and *understanding*. Without
doing this, you will hold onto internal negativity,
and the feminine energy thrives in positivity. If
you want to create inner security for yourself,
then you must let go of as much negativity as
you can.

We can look at things from a negative
perspective or we can choose to take the
positives from it. *Positively processing the past*
starts with fully accepting your past, even
where it hurt you. It's happened and it's done
now. Without being overly emotional, try to look
at the situation in a logical manner.

Look at what position it has left you in. There
will be both positives and negatives. But the
positives will certainly be that you have seen
how resilient you are. You have real-life proof
that you can come through hurtful situations

and stay strong. And I'm sure you have learnt from those experiences too.

Even better, it may have given you awareness of your strengths, as well as any areas of potential improvement. Perhaps you're a girl who lacks the ability to set boundaries. If this has been abused in the past, then you know that this is something to work on.

Next, you must release any bitterness or hate you have. Bitterness sours feminine energy. It brings out a distorted expression of masculinity in such a way that has you being defensive and aggressive. Do not let the experiences you have suffered turn you into a savage. That's not you. That is the pain and hurt being released alongside frustration.

You might feel bitter about men, after having numerous bad experiences, but all this will do is keep you in the frequency that will continue to attract those types of men. Or maybe your bitterness is not directed at any one particular person.

Perhaps you are bitter at society for making you feel bad about your femininity. But the truth is, most of us never stood a chance at being able to embrace our natural state since this society is currently telling us to do the exact opposite.

Whatever it is, you would do better to simply let it go. Doing so is an act of self-love since holding onto negativity only just perpetuates self-pain. And if you are worthy of love, then you do not deserve to continue hurting yourself by holding on to bitterness.

As we said, blame and regret cause wounds to your femininity. Letting go of regret for allowing yourself to be mistreated helps to create a positive space within. Blaming yourself only puts you in a cycle of distrust of your own decisions. Everyone makes mistakes and you are not perfect.

Stopping yourself from blaming others is also powerful, leading us onto our next step which is to drop all victimhood or denial. It's not about blaming yourself or others. It is simply about acknowledging the reality of your past and how each person involved contributed to the situation. If you continue to look at yourself as a victim, you will continue to be one.

You are the hero of your own life, and life is not happening *to you*, it's happening *for you*. Every situation is a lesson, and you are the one in control. Perhaps you had a parent who abandoned you when you were younger and now it has messed up your expression of love or self-worth. Though it was not your fault that this happened, you have the power to fix the damage it caused. The more accountable you become for your own life, the more your life will improve.

Perhaps the hardest step of them all is exercising compassion and forgiveness.

Having compassion for those that have attacked your feminine spirit is difficult, but it will free you from any negativity you hold inside. You can let go of the emotional burdens of stress and frustration.

As the saying goes, *'hurt people hurt people'*. If you had a parent who abandoned you, I can guarantee there was something they suffered in their own development and they didn't fix it, and whatever toxicity that was in them manifested through their treatment of you. They were passing on their unhealed toxicity to you.

In their own way, they too are victims of their own situation. Recognising this is something to be proud of because you are the one breaking the cycle. Few people are able to do this. In fact, depending on what has happened in your past, this may seem impossible right now. If that's the case, it's fine. Don't force it. But doing this helps you to understand why they did what they did, and it helps you to show your inner child that it's safe to play.

Changing your perspective goes a long way. Your inner child has been living in a world of chaos, pain, and fear. But the good thing about the inner world is that it is inside of you, meaning you are the one that gets to decide what state it is in. Continue to work on expressing confidence and letting go of all shame. And understand that you are safe, even if it doesn't yet feel like it.

PRACTICAL EXERCISES

One of the best practical exercises you can do is to write out the wounding experiences you've had and how it makes you feel. If you don't want to get a journal, take time in your day to sit and think about these things. When the feelings come up, do not try to change, or suppress them. Allow yourself to feel and

accept everything that comes up. Just be
aware and accept.

BODY & BEAUTY

Love your body. Everyday commit to showing
appreciation to one different part of your body
or your personal expression of feminine
beauty. One good way to do this is through
mirror work. Sit or stand in front of the mirror
and appreciate your body.

Observe yourself in the mirror and really affirm
to yourself what you love about your
appearance. Look at yourself with admiration
and give yourself positive affirmations. Get
used to complimenting what you like about
your body. When you find yourself criticising
your body, just stop.

Perhaps there are areas of improvement, and
that's okay. You can tell yourself that you will
work on certain aspects without being harsh on

yourself. In the journal, write down things you like about your body.

EMOTIONS

Practice accepting emotions and not over-analysing them. Relax, and feel the emotions as they pass through. As a human, you are an emotional being. But as a woman, you are even more in touch with your emotions. This is something to be proud of. So let go of any shame of your emotional expression.

It doesn't mean to have no emotional control; it simply means that it is unhealthy to suppress emotions for whatever reason. Do daily check-ins (preferably in your journal) by becoming aware of what emotions come up and what situations cause it. If you feel shame around any emotions, track the source of this shame so you can understand why.

SEX & LOVE

Reflect on your relationships. This could be past relationships or even current ones. Be honest with yourself about how you practice sex and love. Take note of the good and the bad.

If you feel you've been mistreated in relationships, ask yourself, *what was it about the experience that attracted/attached you to it?* The answer to this will reveal the issue that needs to be addressed. The more honest, the better.

SELF-WORTH

Taking time to love yourself is the antidote to a society that wants you to be insecure. Write what you love about yourself, your life, your talent and gifts. You should be able to answer "what 3 things do you love about your personality?". Maybe you've never thought about it, but now is the perfect time to.

EMBRACE DIFFERENCES

One of the biggest blocks to your femininity is the mental barrier of thinking that men and women are the same or, even worse, thinking that women should compete with men. This society tends to continuously push the notion that men and women are the same. This is totally false, and it does way more harm than good.

How can you embrace being feminine if you do not proudly accept what it means to be a woman? And being a woman means you are different to a man. In every mammal on the planet, the differences between the **two** genders are clear, and the differences reveal the functions of each gender within that species.

Men and women are not designed with equal qualities, but neither is more important than the other. Women are needed. Men are needed.

Men need women and women need men. Men excel at certain things and women excel at other things. When we bring our differences together, we create the perfect team that empowers all of us.

One of the reasons women today will readily express masculinity is because they are discouraged from expressing femininity in subtle ways. Feminine energy manifests itself in various ways/ behaviours. And those certain behaviours will usually be met with discouragement or judgement from the outside world.

For example, if a woman went on national television and says she does not want to be an independent woman and would prefer a man to take care of her, she is likely to receive a harsh reception. Other women will criticise her. "So don't you have any ambition?", "girl, you can't depend on no man. What if he leaves?" or "Me personally, I could never depend on no man".

Most people have been socially conditioned to participate in gender-role reversal and they unknowingly contribute to the perception of femininity being weak. They take all the bad examples of traditional gender expression and create a narrative that discourages others from being in their natural state. And since none of us want to be considered weak, it makes sense that girls grow up not wanting to be feminine.

It is near impossible for a girl in the Western world to really have a clue about what it means to develop into a feminine woman unless she is lucky enough to be raised in a family that still holds traditional values. Traditional values are attacked. When women embrace masculinity, by declaring they are 'as strong as men' or 'can do anything a man can do', they receive social applause.

After receiving mass social validation from the external world, girls then develop habits that are formed around the expression of masculine energy. For years it may feel mentally good, as the social applause feeds their ego and it feels extremely empowering to be seen as 'a boss bitch', 'a strong woman who can handle it all', 'a fighter who overcomes trauma' and any of the other narratives that some women cling to.

Now, in other cases, that may not have sprouted from chasing social validation. For some girls, it may simply be the life she was born into. Perhaps she grew up in a single-mother family, or unfortunately, she may have become a single mother herself after being abandoned by her child's father. A life of strength and independence may have been forced onto her.

Whatever the case may be though, there is one likely outcome that will manifest: she will soon find that the weight of masculine expression becomes a heavy burden. And she'll find that she no longer wants to play the part of being a man just to fit into society's narrative.

Her instincts drive her curiosity as she wants to embrace femininity. The problem is that it isn't so easy to just change with a finger's click. It's difficult to do this because she may have spent years building up a lifestyle that is based on the masculine persona she was embodying.

Reframe Your View on Femininity

The first step towards embracing femininity is to reframe the beliefs you have about femininity (and masculinity). If you have never intentionally gone on a feminine journey, then I can almost guarantee that much of what you think about femininity is false.

What you would have learned from friends, family, social media and mass media would've been tainted. With this in mind, you must begin this journey by letting go of everything you think you know. Become a sponge soaking in new information.

You must find the areas where you also look down on femininity (this requires great honesty). Reframe these tainted perceptions. Here's one test: if you hear someone say that "women are made to be mothers and wives" do you have a bad reaction to it?

Modern society has indoctrinated girls into taking more pride in the title of 'career woman' than being a mother. Highlighting this doesn't mean that a woman should not have a career if she chooses to have one. But it certainly is not the case that working a job could ever be more satisfying or important than bringing new life into the world and nurturing it to adulthood.

Being career-focused is masculine-centred. Taking pride in being a mother is an expression of the nurturing qualities of the feminine state. There are very few people that even enjoy their jobs and there are very few people that do not enjoy being a parent.

Multiple studies show that around 90% of people are dissatisfied with their job, yet feminist culture pushes the idea that being a career woman is more important than being a mother, and that being raised with the expectation of being a mother is oppressive.

Instead, you have to stop and think about the narratives being pushed onto you. Does the narrative make sense or are you just believing it because it gives you something to fight for? Most of the time, it's the latter.

The majority of the narratives that come from gender role reversal do not make women happy. They just give them a sense of purpose as they fight against what they've been told is oppression. You have to look at things from a fresh viewpoint. Instead of allowing society to spark you into an aggressive mindset, and resisting anything related to traditional roles, you should embrace it.

Femininity is a Power

Femininity is a vulnerable, agreeable, and fundamentally soft state. However, people confuse this with seeing femininity as a state of powerlessness. This is incorrect. And interestingly, it is the greatest female manipulators or most seductive women that know this.

I'm not encouraging you to be manipulative. However, I mention that because if femininity were a state of powerlessness, then it would not be the energy which a manipulator would draw on to influence others. Femininity is a power that is expressed differently than masculinity.

Let's actually consider the definition of the word 'power':

1. *"Ability to act or produce an effect."*

2. *"The capacity or ability to direct or influence the behaviour of others or the course of events."*

People tend to think that the only way to achieve the above two statements is in a masculine way, such as through dominance, aggression, or physical strength. Feminine expression is a state totally capable of achieving these things. You do not have to be masculine to have great influence over other people or your environment. However, it's done in a much different way compared to how a masculine person would try to enact change.

Women are able to use the traits of their femininity to influence others and in certain scenarios, this may even be more powerful than the use of masculinity. Consider that women are naturally better at communication. A woman in touch with her femininity, thus in touch with her innate understanding of non-verbal communication, has more influence than a woman who relies on raw, direct (masculine) communication.

Feminine women are able to 'seed' ideas in a person's mind, allowing the seed to slowly bloom into the result that they desire. The traits of femininity include supportiveness, so she can indirectly encourage people to do what she wants whilst having the person happy and excited about the idea of doing it. The person may even feel that the idea she planted in their mind was actually *their* own idea.

Since femininity is extremely influential, this is an aspect that must be controlled whilst you heal your feminine energy. Many women already use the powers of feminine influence, except they do it from a wounded place. A woman might use her words or her sexuality to manipulate others to get what she wants, and a wounded woman often wants validation from the external world.

Once you heal, you do not need to use your feminine charms to elicit external validation, since the only validation you need will come from within. And a healthy, feminine woman does not need to manipulate to get what she wants.

Femininity is a state of magnetism. A feminine woman's presence is deemed so valuable that it literally inspires people to want to give her value in return. All she has to do is ask for what she wants. Many times, you will not even have to ask – others will *want* to give.

On the other hand, though, a person who tries to exert power in a masculine way might push someone to do what they want to do, using raw directness and dominance. Though it may get the job done, it may not be done in a way where the other person actually wanted to do it.

So I ask you, what is more powerful: to get a person to willingly do what you want or a person who does it because they are being pushed to? If it isn't already clear, femininity is just as powerful as masculinity. It's just in different ways and it's used in different contexts.

EXERCISE

Identify where you rely on others to bring internal value that you should be providing for yourself. This reveals the area of improvement that you have to work on. It may be that you struggle to be without a romantic partner because you do not like being with yourself for an extended period of time.

Or you may use sex as a method to numb yourself from the insecurities that come up when you are by yourself. Whatever it is, know that it's a wound to your femininity and you will be thankful for going through the effort of healing it.

Letting Go of Masculinity

It is one thing to view femininity as a good thing, but it is another challenge when it comes to actually letting go of being masculine. To do this, you must drop all beliefs that you have about masculinity being a state that is better than femininity.

Each state has certain perks, and it is necessary to draw on each energy according to what it is that you are doing. However, you should not have a perception of being 'like men' as being better.

A woman might think that she does not think being masculine is better, but when you observe her actions, words, and the way she thinks, it will tell a different story. For example, a woman who says she doesn't need a man because 'women can do anything a man can do', has now forced herself to pick up the role of being a man. Since the role of the man is indeed necessary, she will now need to embody herself to fill the role.

Proof of this is the fact that women who say they do not need men are the ones most likely to talk, walk, dress, and think like men. Just look at the most radical feminists out there. Though they prove that they will indeed do what men can do, at what cost does it come? It costs them their femininity. Is that a trade you're willing to make? When they attach themselves to masculinity, they consequently drop their femininity, as you cannot be dominantly in both energies at the same time.

However, a better perspective would be this: instead of trying to prove that you can do what a man can do, why not do what a man cannot do? A man can never be feminine like a woman and a woman can never be masculine like a man can be. The design of a woman's body is perfectly suited for the expression of feminine energy and vice versa.

The only reason why some of us seek to be in the opposite energy is that its what society has pushed onto us. When people these days say a woman is "strong and independent", it is a narrative.

If you go back to the origin of where this phrase came from, it came from society pushing it. A woman saying this did not come up with this herself. That idea has been promoted to her. And as we have already said, this society is determined to keep you out of your natural state.

It's not that a woman cannot have strength, but it's that when this is said, they are not talking about the *strength of the feminine*. When they say it, it's coming from a desire to compete with the strength of a man and an admiration for masculine strength.

Though we do live in a time where people cry out for "women empowerment", very few of the people that say this believe in "feminine empowerment". However, by embracing her feminine energy, a woman can be strong in her own right. So, when you say that you want to be strong, it should be out of admiration for femininity and the power that comes with being womanly, not manly.

THE INTERNAL

Expressing Emotions

When embodying femininity, one of the most important milestones of this journey is to connect authentically with your emotions. If you've had experiences that have caused you to feel shame or guilt surrounding your emotional expression, you must make a promise to release it.

Identify those experiences that caused you to feel that way. For different people, it will be different experiences. It could've been that when you were a kid, you may of had a parent tell you that you're being immature for being angry or frustrated. Or perhaps there was a time in class when you hurt your arm and the teacher told you that "you're a big girl and big girls don't cry." Maybe you suffered a harsh breakup and your friends said, "don't be sad, just get someone new".

Even further, you might actually be the one telling yourself that you are weak for feeling certain things or that you should feel uncomfortable for being emotional. Do you feel guilt when experiencing certain emotions? Some women feel guilty when feeling happy. Others may feel shame when intense sadness comes up. Whatever it is that causes you to suppress your emotions, identify it.

Understand that it is necessary to express your emotions. Us humans are an emotional bunch. And women particularly *are* more emotionally expressive than men. Emotional management is not something we are taught today, which is surprising considering that it is such a significant part of our experience here on Earth.

Due to the shame surrounding emotions, being true to your expression may require great vulnerability. It's important to know that being vulnerable requires strength since many people are unable to freely express it. If it was weak, wouldn't it make sense that it's easy to do it? Yet few people can do it. Whether you're a man or a woman, it is a strength to be able to be vulnerable.

For a woman though, this is more significant since women are more emotionally sensitive than men. Many women have been discouraged from accepting this, seeing it as a bad thing. So, they reject this fact. But doing so only robs them of the truth, and thus the ability to find comfort in their femininity.

The traits of the feminine energy include sensitivity, flow, and volatility. This is reflected by the emotions of women that clearly show a capacity for intensity and constant change. However, this is only a bad thing if you see it to be a bad thing. Instead of reacting by saying "Well, men are emotional too", which would be coming from a place of competitiveness, why not be proud of the fact that women are more emotional than men?

Emotions are a beautiful tool that allows us to have a meaningful life. Could you imagine a life without emotions? How boring would that be? Emotions give vibrancy to life. It's the reason why life itself is interesting and intriguing. It's much the reason why your best memories are your best memories. It is the emotions you felt in those past experiences that gave significance to those memories.

So, you should be proud that nature gifted you with the capacity to have a stronger connection to your emotions. You can proudly say "yes, and I love that we are". Do you see how reframing your perspective totally changes the narrative?

I'm not going to deny that it is possible that someone might say "women are emotional" as a way to speak about women in a distasteful way. However, you should not let their negative mindset cause you to look at womanhood in a negative way. When someone tries to make you view the natural state of women in a bad way, do not deny the traits of femininity, embrace it and be proud. Look at *them* as the weird ones for even attempting to attack women in this way.

Accept it, Feel it

Perhaps you are not the type to feel shame for your emotions. However, you may be the type who struggles to embrace your emotions when going through periods of growth, self-reflection or exploring past pains. Oftentimes, we do not like the feelings of discomfort that come when we are trying to move into a new stage of thinking or being.

A good example could be when you are trying to move on from past trauma. In order to *positively process our past,* you must face the fact that the emotions linked to that trauma are going to come up. When you know that this is about to happen, you might shift your perspective or even lie to yourself about the situation to make yourself feel better. Even worse, you might try to not even feel at all.

The problem with suppressing your emotions is that it simply just causes a build-up within. You can never get rid of the emotions that are within you. It is guaranteed that those emotions will come out at some point. But it will reveal itself in an unhealthy way.

When we suppress our feelings, we express them very intensely once we let it out. Working on accepting your emotions helps you to balance them. This stops you from allowing emotions to control you (with outbursts, breakdowns, and having the discipline to walk away from triggering situations becomes easier), as you are in tune with your feelings. And you won't have to engage in certain addictions by trying to make yourself numb to the pain.

An example of suppressing your emotions could be when you are feeling frustrated with your partner, and you do not voice it. The problem doesn't go. It just festers. And when you release it, it will come up so intensely that you may struggle to control it, which inevitably makes the situation worse.

Emotions are there to be felt. It's what connects you to the internal. Accepting your emotions is a part of self-acceptance. It's a part of being authentic. To deny your emotions is to deny a part of yourself. How you feel is *how you feel.* For example, if a certain activity makes you uncomfortable or unhappy but you deny it, you are lying to yourself and the world about who you are and what it is that you're about. Emotions are there to help tap you into your authentic self.

EXERCISE

#1 - When you experience intense emotions, acknowledge it. Simply say what "I feel..." and then say why "...because ......". So, for example, "I feel unhappy like because the boss at work is not highlighting the work I'm putting in".

#2 - Daily check-ins: whether positive or negative, reflect on the significant emotions you felt that day.

#3 - Authentically express without being rude. Do not hide or lie about how you feel to appease others.

Positive vibes

Having a positive vibe is extremely important for femininity. Harbouring a continuous flow of positive emotions creates an internal environment is one in which your inner child feels safe. Make a conscious decision to let go of focusing on negativity. Many of us have attachments to our negative emotions.

We are short-tempered, quick to cuss, quick to get frustrated and quick to judge others. All this does us more than good. It keeps us in fight mode, constantly keeping us in our masculine energy. The feminine state is about letting all of this go.

Don't focus on negativity any more than you need to. Practice being calm-mannered. Prioritise being peaceful and positive. You may feel that you are not naturally like this so it could take time for this to be your natural go-to state. It's worth it.

EXERCISE

Speak to yourself like a little kid when you feel a spurt of aggression or frustration. For example, when you get road rage, in the exact same way that you would speak to a five-year-old say "it's okay. It's not that bad. Just be a little patient and the situation will be fine"

Presence

Another important part of being a feminine woman is living in the present moment. Femininity is about 'being'. It is masculinity that is about 'doing'. And the feminine state is about tapping into the 'internal' whilst the masculine state is heavily fixated on the 'external'. When you are 'present', you are tapped into the experience of your body, rather than living in your head. You are feeling the world through your physical senses.

In the present moment, there are no problems. It is in your mind where all your problem lies. Most problems you have are based on what *could* happen in the future or what has *already* happened in the past. In your head, you think about these potential issues and fears.

You might stress about what could happen if you are late picking the kids up from school or how you will perform at next week's crucial board meeting. Whatever it is, you must ask yourself: is it a problem right *now*? Is it a problem that could happen or might happen? And even if a problem does happen, is it really that big of a deal? And you must also ask, does stressing about the situation make it better? Most of the time the answer is no.

Of course, do not discount potential problems arising. It would be silly to do that. But the point is that you can have the exact same experience with less stress endured. Let go of what could happen or what has happened. Often, you do not have as much control over the situation as you think. Where you do have control, take control. But where you don't, just let go.

When you are in the present moment, you are in the now. And there are usually no problems in the now. You are free from stress and your attention is given to your senses instead. I'll give you an example.

When you go on a vacation, you no longer feel stressed about bills, work, or personal problems. You feel like you're in a totally new world and, in many ways, you are. You are no longer in the world that is your head. You are in your body.

When you are seeing new sights, hearing new things, and you're fully invested in your trip, you are placing yourself in your senses. Your personal problems may still exist, but it doesn't feel that way because your attention is redirected into your body.

But this experience doesn't have to be limited to vacations. You can bring this into your daily living. One of the ways to do this is by cutting out distractions and putting your focus on the present activity or task you are carrying out.

One of the reasons that meditating is such a relaxing experience is because you are doing one thing, and one thing only. You are focusing on your breathing, placing all awareness on that singular task. You are getting the full experience of that one activity. You can carry the same philosophy into daily life.

When you go on a date, be in the experience. Put the phone down, look the person in the eyes and really receive the experience that you are having with the person. Enjoy the sensations that come with the situation and let go of worrying about what you should've done at work earlier, or who you must reply to after. When you spend time with your family, truly take in the experience and be in that moment. The same thing applies to everything else.

Don't spread your attention and energy. Yes, this will certainly require practice. We are constantly blasted with mental distractions in the modern age. Through social media, advertisements and the general duties of everyday life, our minds are being overloaded with new information to process. We are given more distractions than at any other time in human history. It's bound to influence us. However, by embracing presence, we can counteract this.

EXERCISE

#1 - Spot meditations: When you are sitting down (perhaps in a waiting room) or walking to work, practice mini spot meditations. Focus on one physical thing and look at it. Focus on the details of it and put your attention towards it, cutting out everything else.

#2 - Stop and take a second. When you're in 'go-mode' and you can feel yourself becoming frantic, stop and take three deep breaths. Ground yourself and think, what is the next step? And then do that next thing but this time, take your time.

GRATITUDE

Since embracing the internal and expressing positive emotions are important for femininity, one of the best things for feminine development is to work on your gratitude. The traits of the feminine energy are 'receptiveness' and 'openness'.

Consider the sexual design of the female body. The vagina is an open receiver. This is quite clear to see from the physical perspective. However, this same aspect can be translated into other areas of life. Having an open heart and mind allows you to fully receive the experiences that life has to offer.

Gratitude is the state of practising receptiveness in a way that is mentally enjoyable. You begin to look on the bright side of life and you create an internal world of positivity which helps your feminine energy to flow. Every experience serves as a 'giver' of peace, positivity, and pleasure. You just need to be open to it.

It's important to intentionally embrace pleasure and enjoy what you are doing. It isn't enough to just say you want to enjoy life. You must get into the habit of pinpointing the small things that you enjoy.

Perhaps you enjoy the scenery on your way to walk, but when is the last time you *really* appreciated it on the way to work? Did you look at the trees and listen to the birds or were you too focused on the thoughts running around in your mind? You deserve to experience a pleasurable life and you can do so by taking in all these 'small' things.

Receiving

There are many women who have trouble receiving. It seems simple. But sometimes there can be mental obstacles that prevent this and one of the major roadblocks to receiving is a lack of self-worth. Or a better way of putting it would be a lack of being able to recognise your self-worth because you definitely have value even if you can't see it yet. You just need to believe it.

The value of *The Feminine* is inherent, and this is why women tend to attract favours, gifts and assistance from the external world more so than men. When you feel inherently valuable, you see it as natural to receive value back from the world. It simply feels like an equal exchange. If you find yourself struggling to receive, then take some time out to remind yourself that you are worth the value which is being given. Positive affirmations go a long way.

When the world offers you value, take it and be thankful. Do not question it. To question it would be to question yourself. This means, that when someone offers you a compliment, do not downplay it.

Don't say "oh I'm not looking that good today" when someone at the office tells you that you look amazing. Simply say "thank you". And when you say, "thank you", do not robotically say it simply out of habit. Truly *feel* thankful as this is the beneficial part of practising gratitude.

When a man offers to help you, accept it (if the situation is safe and reasonable of course). Perhaps you are trying to carry a furniture delivery up to your apartment, if your partner or friend offers to help, kindly accept the offer. This is one of the perks of being a woman: people are willingly available to assist you.

But then comes the next step and this is where many will struggle: rather than just accepting help, be okay with asking for help when you know you need it. One of the reasons people (both men and women) struggle to ask for help is because they feel inferior when they acknowledge that they may not be enough to complete a task by themselves.

Asking for help does not decrease your worth. It just means you understand the power of teamwork. It also shows that you accept that you are stronger in some areas more than in others. To ask for help without triggering that feeling of inferiority means you *have to* drop your ego. This is a good thing since such an ego is doing more to hurt than help.

Why make things harder than it needs to be, especially when they can be easy? It doesn't mean offloading your responsibilities onto others, but it does mean that you have the chance to lighten the load on yourself. And this extends to so many areas, including:

- Accepting leadership in a relationship so that you can allow him to take on more responsibilities

- Allowing men to take control of the date so that you can let go and relax

- Gaining new knowledge from someone who knows more about a subject

- Getting assistance at work so that you are not as stressed

And much more

Celebrate Yourself

Another aspect of being grateful is celebrating your accomplishments. This means that you celebrate what you've been through, who you are and even just making it this far. Whether you know it or not, you've been through a lot just to make it to this point in your life. You should feel proud. You should be appreciative of all the good you've done and all the results you've achieved.

You may have been through an abusive relationship with a narcissist or been abandoned as a kid or you've suffered from being shamed for who you are, but you are still here surviving. *Be proud.*

And if you are thriving, having made great achievements then make sure to stop and truly sit in that moment to celebrate your wins. This is nothing to be made light of. When people highlight your wins, do not downplay them.

It doesn't mean you should be arrogant or act as if you are better than everyone else. But it certainly means you should not resist being acknowledged for the success you've had. When someone says, "it's so amazing that you started a yoga class that now has over a hundred monthly students!", don't say "oh it's nothing". Say "I appreciate that. It was hard work!" Acknowledge your wins.

SELF CARE

Take Time For Yourself

One of the most important aspects of femininity is taking the time out to indulge in self-care, which means to take care of the internal. The hustle and bustle nature of today's Western society typically dampens feminine energy. This culture is heavily focused on independence, ruthless climbing of the corporate ladder and always being in 'go-mode'.

Yes, it is respectable for anyone to be able to make things happen. However, the feminine state is not just about 'doing'. If you only just 'do', you are very likely to drain yourself. View taking time out for yourself as just as important as working is. Because it is.

Being in 'go-mode' all the time can induce huge amounts of pressure and with pressure comes stress. Relaxation is key for letting this all go away, adding balance back into your world. Carve out periods where you can do nothing and just 'be', or you can do things that bring pure enjoyment.

Don't get caught up always having to do something or needing to do something to "feel productive". Find a time to be still and present, this is productive for your spirit. Perhaps just laying down and listening to relaxing music or watching a movie (keyword: relaxing). You can even find time to take walks. Take slow, soothing breaths and enjoy the environment. Slowing things down like this helps you to draw the joy out of life. Dedicate time towards letting go of all control, perfectionism, and worries.

Self-care is more than just forcing yourself to take a break. It's a practice of self-love. You must believe that it's worth it. You are not just 'spending' your time when you put it towards self-care, you are investing it, and the great thing is that this particular investment yields a healthy return.

See it as an investment in the satisfaction of your daily life experience. When you take time to yourself, you recharge yourself in a way that allows you to exert more energy afterwards anyway.

Love your body

As the saying goes, your body is your temple. If this statement is true, then it means your body should be treated with the gentleness, reverence, and respect that any temple is. When you mistreat it, you mistreat yourself – in mind and spirit. The same applies when you allow it to be mistreated by others.

Take a moment to be honest with yourself and ask: *are you treating your body with the love it deserves, both externally and internally? Are you appreciating your body? Are you looking at it with love and admiration, proud of what God gave you?* Or are you looking at the bodies of others wishing yours was like theirs?

Your body is *your* personal expression of *your* beauty. Regardless of where you are at on your physical/health journey, decide right now that your body deserves your love. It doesn't need it from anyone else but you. This doesn't mean you shouldn't improve it. It simply means you should let go of the shame surrounding it.

Once you do this, seek to show it even more love by working out, eating healthy and applying appropriate skin care. These are all acts of self-love with the added bonus of nurturing your beauty. Your love of your body will grow the more work you invest into it. It's easier to feel like a beautiful feminine woman when your body is being looked after.

It's important to heal the disconnection between you and your body, seeing it as a teammate helping you to have the best experience in this physical reality. Once you see your body as important, you will not allow people to misuse, abuse or mistreat it. You will not allow those that are not worthy enough to have access to it.

EXERCISE

Another way to show appreciation to your body is by doing a gratitude meditation. But in this meditation, you are going to go through different parts of your body and literally thanking them for serving you. Thank your organs individually. Thank your legs for allowing you to walk. Thank your fingers for making life easier. Thank your eyes for giving you sight. Thank each body part.

Be selective

Let's dive deeper into the saying "your body is your temple". By saying that your body is the temple, you are saying that it houses your spiritual body. It is the home of your energy.

Self-care is not just about taking care of your physical body, but also your spiritual body too. The assets of this temple include your time, attention, and your energy.

The key to taking care of these assets is being selective with it. Anything of high value is not easily accessible. The rarer something is, the more expensive it is — like a pure, polished diamond. The more expensive something is, the fewer amount of people can have it. That's how you should see your attention, time, and energy. Put a high price on your worth and then justify that price.

Be selective about who and what you allow having access to you. This includes people, partners and even the products/content you consume. The trick is to give out energy to things and people who return positive value back to you.

Being selective with these assets empowers your nurturing side. If you keep giving out energy without a return on investment, you'll drain yourself. And consequently, there is less for you to give back to the world.

You also have to put an end to people pleasing. Ask yourself: do you prioritise other people's fulfilment over yours? Is it uncomfortable for you to set healthy boundaries? Do you value other people's thoughts over your own? Are you constantly going hard for others and not yourself? These are all important questions to ask.

However, people who are naturally very giving should never feel bad about being this type of person. Instead, you should be *very* selective with who gets this side of you. Remove yourself from toxic situations, keep toxic people out of your life and refrain from being in toxic environments that threaten the flow of your feminine energy.

Stop being with partners who do not care about your satisfaction. Many times, a girl might focus heavily on what a guy can do for her on a superficial level, or on if he's able to stimulate her emotionally or sexually.

She might totally ignore how this person treats her on a deeper level or even if he actually cares about her. If you stay in situations where the person is showing an outright lack of care, it will reaffirm to your mind that you are not someone worth caring about. So, kill this weed before it even has a chance to grow.

The only plant you want growing in your environment is the beautiful flowers of positive affirmations. Prioritise friends, family and partners that contribute to you being the confident, healthy, feminine, and fulfilled woman you want to become. This goal comes before anything. If they are an obstacle to you becoming the woman you dream about, they do not deserve to stay in your world.

EXERCISE

Get rid of old belongings to signify change: one ritualistic action you can take to help you start this journey is to reshuffle your home and get rid of things that do not serve you. This could mean changing your home's interior design. Throwing out old clothes and buying new ones. Letting go of these things will make space for the new character that's about to come.

CONCLUSION

Softening the shell

We live in a world where the state of everything is currently unbalanced. For years, you've been taught the opposite of what you needed to learn. Most of us have been forced to be hard to survive. The most beautiful thing about beginning your femininity journey is the pain it will alleviate, the peace it will bring and the pleasure you will feel.

Healing your feminine energy brings a sense of inner freedom. You can let go of many things. For you, that may be letting go of control. For others, it could be letting go of fears. For many, it will be letting go of the mask you have put on; you can finally be your true, authentic self.

This is a journey. This is not a journey that will take one day. It will take many days. But that is the beautiful thing. As you embark on this journey, the pleasures and powers of The Feminine will continuously reveal themselves.

You will start attracting what you want. Men will begin to treat you differently and the quality of men you attract will change. Even more, the men *you* become attracted to will change. Your friends might change or even the job you do might have to change. You will begin to have realisations about why certain things took place in your past and you'll gain a sense of control over how to shape your reality to be how it was meant to be.

God did not design women to be inherently unsatisfied in their natural state. It is quite the opposite. If you follow the confusion of modern Western culture, then you're likely to be dissatisfied. Embedded in nature's way is the code to fulfilment. And as you grow, you will become impressed with what's in store for a healed feminine woman.

Remember, a woman's greatest strength is her womanhood. Her greatest power is her femininity, and it is that which she should take the most pride in. You've got this.

EXERCISE

Identify improvements. You've went through your best traits, but what are some qualities that you can improve on? Accountability is not your enemy. It's one of your best friends.

You may love yourself as you are, and that's great. But think about how much more you would love yourself once you improve. Be honest with yourself and accept the things you need to work on. Write it down and check in every month to track your progress.

ENDING PAGE

This information is only a small step into the journey of feminine development – so you can flourish in your feminine. These are designed to be easy-to-digest books that cover only a few topics. There is much more to femininity that was not covered in this book, such as connecting to nature, setting boundaries or how to relate to a masculine man. But this is a gradual journey, and not a quick race, so I intentionally left more to be discovered in the future volumes of this 'Femininity Series'.

I hope to see you in the next volume but until then I'll say this: *take great pride in your womanhood*. Never accept the notion that femininity is something to shy away from. These are lies that prevent you from living in alignment and fulfilment. As I've shown you, the expression of feminine energy is amazing.

If there are any specific topics you would like me to include in the future volumes, then you can email me at: ReemusBailey@GMAIL.com or comment/message on one of my social media accounts: @Reemusb (TikTok & Instagram)

.

Made in the USA
Coppell, TX
09 November 2022

86096557R00049